I0756292

FINISHING LINE PRESS
www.finishinglinepress.com

Urban Trout

poems by

Jevin Lee Albuquerque

Finishing Line Press
Georgetown, Kentucky

Urban Trout

ISBN 979-8-89990-364-9 First Edition

ACKNOWLEDGMENTS

Desk Job published in *Fish Food Magazine*
Less Inclined in *Paradise Review*
Street Soldiers in *ArLiJo* and *Monterey Poetry Review*
Saloonatics in *Literary Juice Magazine*
Throwin'em Back and Urban Trout in *The American Journal of Poetry*
High Octane/State of the Union in *Poussières Du Monde, Paris, France*
Keyboard Fresh in *Haight Ashbury Literary Journal*
The Writing Group in *Borderline* and *Livid Squid*
Spider-rat in *VerbalArt*
Henry "Gangsta" Miller Valentine in H*omestead Review*
Jackson Square in *StepAway Magazine*
Rock Creek in *Spillway* and *Monterey Poetry Review*
Z-Bop in *Apeiron Review*
HM in *Monterey Poetry Review*

Thank you, Mom, Dad, Uncle, Katieann, JL, BT, RS, JLF, JH for the endless support and for taking this journey with me.

Publisher: Leah Huete de Maines
Editor: Christen Kincaid
Cover Art: Tonni Albuquerque
Author Photo: Jevin Lee Albuquerque
Cover Design: Elizabeth Maines McCleavy

Order online: www.finishinglinepress.com
also available on amazon.com

Author inquiries and mail orders:
Finishing Line Press
PO Box 1626
Georgetown, Kentucky 40324
USA

Contents

Desk Job

Nail me to a f--ing desk
right hand, bone crush, finger
left, the middle

Hands pulse, blood pour
nail, feet, the floor

Burn eyes, techie
facebook flashdance
dollar, white-human-blood-suck
nail pounder

Knotty-neck-fat-belly-health-riddle
less lived, each day
sleepless, Grim-reaper-bedmate

(Check)

Decay, jobless desk job
blood oil, blood boil

Experimental rattrap

I'm pulling hands free
finger
table
bloody feet

Less Inclined

To slip into
The mainstream
Cigarette in mouth
Most hours
Minutes
Seconds
Wait a second
Another fix
Tweak
Of wardrobe
Blue shoes
Blue shirt
Brothers
Getting
Out of car
Flossing
Into Salem Liquor
Two strong
One
To
Organ—ize
For you
A bag
Fix
What you need
To get through
The day
A cloudy
Summer day
Here in these
Streets of San Francisco
North Africa
Africa's dream
Machine
To take care of
Your needs

Late night
Or day
This is the loin
Tender
Like steak
To entice
You to
Believe
You are O.K.

Street Soldiers

shopping for a cart
street soldier, former
Vi-etcetera
said red tides
flown in jungles
blown, into stars
orbiting, out of mind
stars in hand, mouth
a cookie-crispy-bomb-exploding
stars die
red tide consumes
blood jungles
drowning monkeys
toucans, wild boar
bare the truth
I wasn't there
here, street soldiers
carts in hand

Reno

Blurred, crooked streets, stroll
jaded hookers, cellulite, cell phone
out-in, shady motels, music
in the parking lot?

Swimming pool, holding on, can't keep
holding on, filth, smoke-filled
Casinos, no-no's, it's all
wrong for a free drink

"I'm sentenced today, what does
it matter if I have a gun in my
pack? Nothing matters, call you back
baby"

My back burns, sun
reclined ladies, getting on
been, getting on, years

Plastic-surgery-affected
only half, half lips
one cheek lifted
droop down

Goin' down, drain slip
pool, underwater
vacuum

Hands up, final breathe
street-casino-slurp
Restore the fish

Saloonatics

Saloonaticking time bombs
Arms spun back
Blues hazing
Clocks explode
Roman numerals floating
Purple hazing clouds above the disheveled
Downtrodden and beat memories engraved
The bar
Hard wood
Dance floors
Whores
Earrings jingle
Gum plucked
Chewed into past
Hooked on Roman Numerals
Floating
Sipped Mayflies
June
A little too late

Throwin'em Back

Nothing good happens

In a bar poet

Thief   stoner   whore

Torn livers

Trade stories

Mushrooms
Cosmic

Downtrodden

D
O
W
N
S
T
R
E
A
M
E
R
S

Hoping

for
one
more
spawn

Urban Trout

Fish trippin' over myself
The-old-reliable 50-bucker
Hotel town ten
Minutes fly-fish-river
Urban wild trout
Consumed by pike-musky
Splash next room
Below: gold chained
fellow
tvs stereos
Door-slam-skinhead
Stairs: walking dead-meth-jesus
Blanketed, shopping cart full
Cigarette-burned-down
Lips, greet you stares
No stars
Gang-runnin-hustle
Hookers
Exchange your room quick
Sheets reveal cigarette
Burns bodies
Walls pock-marked
Door trap next abode
bathroom-stained
Outsider
Make a break for it
In time
slide-by-meth-jesus
Into my soul
Less this hotel
2am, drivin' dirty

High Octane/State of the Union (2014)

On the outside I have a window
bows, bends, extreme conditions
opened, observations, wind on face
eyes sticky smog, Los Angeles
Descending, worn out, working
for minimum, what a breeze
blows the state of things
Health careless efforts made
blood shed, congressional old men
My side, your side
bi-polar system
why play the game
Broken winds blown, ash green eyes
whirlwinds, poverty, immigration
foreign, lack of understanding
for years, pay the price
at the pump, oil my joints
Getting old, the young nation, fighting
the enemy, greenies, semi-automatic
wielding, wilted debate, bi-polarized
again and again, worn out hooker state

Railroad to the Theatre (Madrid, New Mexico)

the theatre is ours
belongs to lovers
undone in seats
cushioned for drama
drums pound

native-spanish-french
        poesía
lush deserts chew stars

stars   never-enough
skin   pleasure

drunk   for the road
tripped-on   warriors

        minds

bodies   takeover   the railroad
rush…   to the Gods!

why wait   we see
power   consumed
spirit-attach-hungry

    new-art
                gifted in ways
                                the other

quick-french-tongue
seduct angels
sing in your hair

castanets   click
teeth   doors open
we drift   s t r e a m s

desert fauna embarrassed
too rugged for acceptance
shoulders turned to the sun

our warriors black
snakes side
slither wither bless
us an ounce hope venom

un-damned we sip kisses
trout fabled waters
whisper there she
goes A l b u q u e r q u e

Keyboard Fresh

I see you up there
key-bored waitress
night away flu
sick with rhythm
but still the males
always showin' trumpet
shoot me   E   male
my rhythms   are
blowin'   free-me-up   let
meee,   be   be   beat
I'm happenin' in this hood
away from   kitchen
greassssse   glass-slap-table
cold coffee   café
drum   me   up
after hours,   your
bass   too   cool
fools in the way
show a lady a   goooood   time
drum   me   fun
belly-long-gone
see me
  me   for what I
am   not   yours

The Writing Group

Why engage God when you can sit
        In a writing group
Suck the marrow out of your brother
        Violate your sister
Splash around in a pool of blood
        Showing off each other's fangs
The loudest voice wins, there
        Must be a winner
        And a loser
Whatever you do speak loud
        Drown out the loser
The one who makes you, claustrophobic
The one with the, non-MFA prose
        She must die
How dare she sit in silence
        Write with fire
Melting ice-cycles in each hand
Ready to stab my little heart
Already shattered a million times
How dare she write with God

Hummus

Jazz
Café
Eating Hummus
You   L O V E   Hummus
It's been so long
Since we ate
Rabbit food
Without you   I still eat
Not the same
Opinions
Death   Hummus
I gorge down Hummus
You spread it light
Ballerina
Death   tongue
Greeting Hummus
Slowing-down-time
I miss

Spider-rat

Spider-awake-sleep
Odd hours
Mice-rat-rage

Cheese phobia
Snap
        Back
                Snap

Fur sandwich
Web-sticky-bed
                Slept

Arachno-rats-mice
                        Scene
Night seen
                Bed
        Walls

Crisis-room-climb

        Dreams

(Oh, wonderful dreams)

Henry "Gangsta" Miller Valentine

Ocean pristine
Meet Watsón, ese
Dark lot, parking

"Can you give me a ride?"
        Tattoo arm blaze
                Eye twitch
        "My girlfriend left me on Valentine's, ese"

"Nah, man, I live close by"

Step
        Northside

                Southside

        Emotion-less

Knocks

Waves   Big Sur

                        Desperation

        Reminder

Check your wallet

Naked-Esalen-bodies

        Gangsta

Sippin'

        Oranges

        of

Hieronymus Bosch

Jackson Square

Stuffed-up environs, the non-poetic
Washed-up, silence
Boredom, despair, undone
Until: horns bless dirty streets
Alcohol, the tongue
Minds washed in gutters
Of brass, where beauty is found

Rock Creek

Today I returned to my campsite

No critters footprints

Alone

But rocks, near the fire pit

In a line

Painted: yellow-blue-white-orange

The work of a small person

Hope

The daughter we never had

Z-Bop

Walkin' the Quarter, New Orleans
          Ghost of Z-bop
          regular, drum
          Mississippi talkin'
                    beats non-stop

Birds say hi: "Can you hear that bird, talkin'?
                              He's talkin' to me
                    Hey Darlin', how bout a dollar?
          Crazy last night, clubbed by the cops"

White boy stare, Z-bop's swollen eye

"Darlin', sing you a happy birthday song,
          for a little tip
Go 'head mudslide
          let that steel guitar rip
Hey man
          hold that one, boy
Damn, you white
          keep that beat
          lesson for free
          few extra tips
One your white girls
          For me,
                    Bruthaaa"

Big smile, ratatatat
          "That's it now,
                    Hold that beat…
                              Hey pretty little thing:
          Check out my poor feet"

Holes in socks, calloused hands,
          Wiggling toes
          The ladies man

Monterey Transit Plaza

wheel

chair

strapped-legs
d
o
w
n

"nice brim, man"

da man, complement

my day brother

(smile)

remote cruise along
sparks

Bar Mechanic

build-bikes gangs

twelve-a-month

year   make model

myself   business

protected   not-in

leather   girls

    hot-drug-rings

sip-trout   mayflies

The Poet

Tough living
        Bottom shoe
                        Gum stuck

Sculpin shelf
        b
        u
        b
        b
        l
        e
        s
                blown

Help the needy
        You are one
                of them

HM

Henry Miller
Talk to your boy your girls
Around the world poverty train

tracks wind

Upside-down-spent-spinners
tents
trees
books
literary

Sinners

Old Testament Rebellion

Selling your

Nin-game-endless

Old master

Tip's

Worked at Tipitina's

Cook   Clean
          Cook   Clean

Gator catchin' morn'

          Bait 'em on land

14 footer on
       a
          c
            h
              a
                i
                  n
                              dinner

Neighbor

Ah, you're a poet now

you
      want
                to
                    borrow

5 bucks

Jevin Lee Albuquerque grew up in Santa Cruz, California, fishing and chasing a soccer dream. He played Division 1 soccer and earned a degree in Latin American Studies from UCLA. Soccer took him around the world as a professional player and his travels sparked the desire to become a writer. He's been nominated for the Pushcart Prize and was a semi-finalist in the Faulkner—Wisdom Competition. He's published dozens of shorts stories and poems both in the United States and abroad. Jevin's work has been translated into French by Bernard Turle in the collectif, *Poussières Du Monde* (Éditions François Bourin, 2014). His poetry has appeared in *Universal Oneness*—Poetry Anthology (Authorspress, New Delhi, India, 2020). He learned how to write and perform poetry in North Beach, San Francisco, to jazzy-free-speech-rhythms. If not writing or working with kids to improve their soccer skills, he can be found fly-fishing for trout, spey casting for steelhead or hiking with his partner in Big Sur.

www.ingramcontent.com/pod-product-compliance
Lightning Source LLC
LaVergne TN
LVHW090541110826
845146LV00003B/1220

* 9 7 9 8 8 9 9 9 0 3 6